THE FUNDAMENTAL BIBLICAL AND COUNSELING PRINCIPLES For CHRISTIAN MARRIAGE

Paul Adomako-Mensah

Copyright © August 2020

ISBN : 978 – 1– 61957 – 001 – 6

Unless otherwise indicated, all scripture quotations are taken from the Holy Bible, New Living Translation, copyright by Tyndale House.

Contact details

Layout and Cover Design by 0242539261

Printed by OKAB. USA

Dedication

This book is dedicated to all Christians especially those who are yet to choose their lifetime partners, married couples, and those in the field of marriage counseling.

Acknowledgment

I thank the Almighty God for His mercies and grace which is always abundant to his people for giving me the knowledge, direction, opportunity, and strength to write this book. I wish to express my special thanks to all sources consulted for the information listed in the reference. Special thanks also go to Dr. Jennings Boateng for his contribution and editing. Finally, to Susana my dear wife, and all the children Nathaniel, Emmanuel, and Susan for their moral support, typing, and prayer in writing this book.

Content

Dedication	iii
Acknowledgment	iv
Foreword	7
Introduction	12

CHAPTER ONE

The Concept of a Christian Marriage 21

What is marriage and (its meaning) ....…….. 21

Significance and purpose of marriage ....…..…..… 24

The foundation of the institution of marriage….....…..… 26

CHAPTER TWO

The Fundamental Guiding Principles in Choosing a Lifetime Partner 29

Wrong reasons for marriage 29

Right reasons for marriage………………………….....… 30

Factors to be considered in preparation towards marriage... 31

Choosing a partner when "ready" 33

Ask God in prayer 34

Choose a believer like you and not an unbeliever 35

Talk to your Christian parents/guardian/pastor ………….. 36

Suggestion from close individuals................................ 37
Other important factors for consideration.................... 37
Making the move.. 38
What if it does not work... 39
If both agree.. 40
What to do next (Get Married) 41

CHAPTER THREE
The Principles of a Christian Marriage longevity 45
Reasons that Contributes to Rampant Divorces............... 45
Oneness in Christian Marriage....................................... 48
Transparency in Christian Marriage................................ 50
Adaptability in Christian Marriage.................................. 51
Serving in Christian Marriage.. 53
Love and Submission in Christian Marriage..................... 54
Couple Responsibilities towards their Family................... 61
Fidelity in Christian Marriage... 63
Communication in Christian Marriage............................. 66
Forgiveness in Christian Marriage................................... 68
The Couples Christian Spirituality................................... 69

Conclusion 71
References 74

Foreword

Then working as an attending Physician in Ghana, I was quite flabbergasted when my Nurse alerted me a patient (lady) I was going to examine was a virgin. Until then I had implicitly presumed there would not be and that 26-year-old virgins were nonexistent! How wrong I was! No wonder I was as described, greatly astonished. My mistake was: I have NOT traveled the world around, and certainly cannot see the whole globe (world) at the same time as the Omnipresent God. Yet I had considered it extinct or perhaps have equated the probability of 26-year old virgin being in existence (on earth), let alone meeting one, to the likelihood of finding a human being on Pluto! Called it presumption, preconception, or perhaps prejudice but I did change my mind and have changed it since then.

The fact that your perception of the world we live in is based on information (knowledge) of things, events, and people does not mean you couldn't be mistaken (as I was) in your worldview. Your sources of information (the news, the various media, movies, studies, work, cultures, expeditions, researches, etc.) could errantly affect your perspective to think that evil (sin) has defeated good, and, that divorce has swallowed up a good marriage. Or that, there could NOT be any married couples or families living the prescription (precepts) of God (the designer of marriage) as pertains to marriage. Oh yes, REAL couples and families are living out the God-ordained principles and in the fullness of the purpose of God for marriage, representing, declaring and proclaiming if you would, a glimpse of the ultimate consummation of the Church (Bride of the lamb) and Jesus Christ (the groom). I am talking about countless couples who have defied the odds (so-called divorce norm: "if it doesn't work, that's what divorce is there for"). These take their wedding vows seriously, and meet **any** and **every** challenge and threat head-on, to not only defeat them but also use them as stepping stones to strengthen their relationship. Like your muscles, if a "severe" workout (threat) doesn't destroy them it strengthens them.

    Family, as the unit of society but more so a design of God, and is by its very existence insurmountable threat to the Devil! No wonder he is doing everything to destroy (infidelity, irreconcilable differences, selfishness/unwillingness to sacrifice, inordinate ambitions, homosexuality, etc.) and deface marriage. Marriage, and for that matter the family, continuously reminds the devil of his ultimate defeat and demise. This is the spiritual etiology of the desecration and degradation of the institution of marriage. This is a call to action, responsibility, and accountability for married and prospective couples. You thought you had issues? Well, get married and you would recognize you've NOT seen anything yet! This is not to scare or dissuade you from getting married but to give you heads up. And that's the reason for this booklet.

My Pastor, confidant, and friend, Rev Paul Adomako-Mensah, a gifted, expository and fervent Teacher, Writer, Educator, and Pastor have done an impressive job with the pages of this booklet. Firstly, by properly diagnosing the ill-notion of the fear of entering (into), and of the deteriorating and petrifying conditions prevalent in marriages today that dominate the headlines of resources likely and commonly used by people for information on the subject (that make prospective couples scared) but secondly and more importantly, providing biblical and experiential solutions to the subject. What Rev. Adomako-Mensah has done is KISS! *Keep It Simple and Stupid*. The principles expounded in this guidance booklet when adhering to would surely empower old, new, and prospective couples to "stick together", and with their invitation of the Holy Spirit into whatever and every situation, would be assured the victory of the longevity of their marriage. (Eccl. 4:12).

Divorce is NEVER the answer to any marriage problems! In my evaluation and opinion, no one wins in divorce. It is a BIG LIE and DECEPTION from the Devil. Moreover, God the Creator of the universe hates Divorce (Mal. 2:16). Divorce is a contemporary LIE of legally-supported demonstration and display of Violence, Betrayal, Covenant-breaking, Selfishness, Self-lovingness, Treachery, Humiliation, Thanklessness, Unforgiveness, but more importantly a LIE (from the Devil) and an abomination and profanity in the eyes of God. I would NOT forget to mention the trauma of emotional pains (Which the strongest opioid cannot mitigate), hurts, animosity, Rancor, etc., that accompany divorces

I think Rev. Adomako-Mensah has, through the pages of this booklet demonstrated unprecedented compassion. Compassion is not only empathizing with a pathetic situation but also doing something to correct it! It is compassion that drove Jesus Christ, the Creator of the universe, the ONLY Potentate, King of kings and Lord of lords, my personal Lord, King, Redeemer, Savior, Father, and Master, to leave his

Throne and Divinity to take human form to come and rescue man (me). Pastor Adomako-Mensah has noted the downward spiraling of the unit of society, the family, and has succinctly offered proven principles and guidance that if applied, shall overcome every pressure that marriage would ever be subjected to. Since they're biblical principles, they transcend over and across every human endeavor and societal classifications. Pastor Adomako-Mensah has bravely and boldly tackled the uncertainty, "un-confidence" and unsureness of finding the right partner by offering practical instructions to help you find your GEM. How would the prospective couples avoid temptations while preparing themselves until the wedding day? Excellent practical guidance is provided on this.

Because of the purpose and uniqueness of marriage, it's inconceivable that an all exhaustive and complete knowledge could be acquired and, especially, be presented in such a small booklet. Marriage is the only relationship in which sexual intercourse is permitted, where two people can become one flesh, and where all the four types of love (*Eros, Philia, Storge,* and *agape*) confluent and thrive. What this means is that no two marriages are the same in the same way as Jesus Christ uniquely relates to each believer in Him. What this booklet has done is to give the foundational principles for prospective couples and couples to build their relationship with the uniqueness of their God-given resources to fulfill their purpose. Well implemented, your relationship would flourish and grow, and you would harvest the good fruits love, joy, selflessness, patience, maturity, satisfaction, fulfillment, etc., of your labor. Marriage is for you—to make you the BEST you! God blesses. God bless you, Rev Adomako-Mensah for this work to glorify God, and Thank you for the privilege to write the foreword to this family-saving and kingdom-building work.

Dr. Jenning Boateng
(MD, MSc. MSF & MBA, Maranatha Prayer line Ministry)
Vergennes, Vermont (USA) November 2018

Introduction

We are living in a perverse society where good has turned to evil and evil promulgated as good. The writer of the Psalms wrote "You love evil more than good, lying rather than speaking righteousness" (Ps. 52:3). Kenneth L. Barker and John R. Kohlenberger III penned that "The values of the wicked are completely distorted. They love anything twisted, perverted, and corrupt. Falsehood and aggressive words aim at the undoing of others. They stand for whatever is against God's standards of goodness and righteousness."[1] The prophet Isaiah also gave a strong warning to humanity that "Woe to those who call evil good, and good evil; who put darkness for light, and light for darkness; who put bitter for sweet, and sweet for bitter" (Isa. 5:20). No wonder the apostle Paul

---

[1] Kenneth L Barker and John R. Kohlenberger III, T*he Expositor's Bible Commentary Abridged Edition Old Testament* (Grand Rapids, Michigan: Zondervan, 1994), 855.

warned Timothy that in the last day's people will be lovers of themselves, without self-control, despisers of good, and lovers of pleasure rather than lovers of God (2 Tim. 3:1-4), which the church need to turn away from them. Our society is dominated by so much departure from the truth and all that is God that the very first divine institution established by God (Marriage) has been corrupted with human fallacies. In nearly every major Christian denomination, God's laws regarding marriage, divorce, sexuality, and gender differences are being discarded and replaced with an acceptance of the most corrupt human practices. Among the major denominations, clergy divorce and remarriage are hardly an issue. As *Time* magazine aptly describes today's religious landscape, "Denomination that once would not tolerate divorced ministers now find themselves debating whether to accept avowed lesbian ones."[2] Marriage, which is the unit and building block of society has now been abused by society itself. The sanctity of marriage as pertains to Scripture has been taken to the mud. The unfortunate situation is that the world is setting the standards of how and what marriage should be. Today, people are living as couples without proper marriage rituals. Improper marriage

---

[2] Alexander Strauch, *Biblical Eldership, An Urgent Call to Restore Biblical Church Leadership* (Littleton, CO: Lewis & Roth Publishers, 2016), 75.

has been sugar-coated to the extent that people think there is nothing wrong with "boy-girl friendship", "domestic partners", "roommates", living together and engaged in sexual activities as couples, etc. The most serious and abominable of all is the "same-sex" (homosexuality)[3] marriage which has widely been accepted at national levels and incorporated into most developed countries' constitutions as an acceptable norm. The sad thing about it is that those countries that spearheaded or heralded Christianity to most parts of our world have now become a stab at Christ back. Example, United Kingdom, United States, and Germany. Christian teachings on virtues, morals, and Godly values which were once introduced in school curriculums have now been relegated to the backyard. Ministers of the gospel who have been entrusted with the message of God rarely teaches the subject of marriage in their pulpits, if not at marriage ceremonies, you barely hear marriage sermons. Most young to-be-couples who lack the fundamental teachings of marriage are at the crossroad or dilemma, do not know what to do and where to get help, hence, lack of fundamental biblical and counseling principles of marriage seems to have contributed to rampant divorces, immoral and

---

[3] A Sexual Relationship Between Two Members of the Same Sex. Tremper Longman III, *The Baker Illustrated Bible Dictionary* (Grand Rapids, Michigan: Baker Publishing Group, 2013), 796.

promiscuous life of partner(s) evident in adultery, fornication, homosexuality, chronic diseases, HIV AIDS, suicidal attempts, depression, truant children, animosity, grief, bad-temperament, and the like. These consequences predominantly appear to have harmed couples, the Church, the society, and the nations as well.

The question now is, should Christians or the church allow the world to determine what the standard of marriage should be? Should we allow society to indoctrinate our children and the generations yet unborn with the worldly perverted standards of marriage? There is even a rumor spreading like a wildfire brainwashing people concerning the choice of gender—people would have to decide the choice of the gender they want irrespective of their natural and birthed ones. Is gender now turning into relativism?[4] Or has it become difficult to find the difference between light and darkness? Or the dichotomy of rain and draught? If Christians, theologians, biblical scholars, ministers of the gospel would keep quiet without addressing the evil standards of the society regarding

---

[4] Relativism, roughly put, is the view that truth and falsity, right and wrong, standards of reasoning, and procedures of justification are products of differing conventions and frameworks of assessment and that their authority is confined to the context giving rise to them. Or a view that ethical truths depend on the individuals and groups holding them. Stanford Encyclopedia of Philosophy, https://plato.stanford.edu/entries/relativism/ accessed 01/24/2019.

the sanctity of marriage, our descendants, and the generations yet unborn would be misled. Future generations of Christian marriages would be in chaos, the rate of divorce would skyrocket, and God and posterity would never forgive those entrusted to speak and teach the true Word of God.

To address the issue at stake, this study is embarking on the study of 'The fundamental Biblical and Counseling Principles in Christian Marriage.' The purpose of this study is to help educate, inculcate and prepare our young Christian children, to-be-couples, deficient couples, members in our churches, and future generations for marriage and its longevity with the fundamental biblical and counseling principles of marriage. Indeed, as secondary sexual characteristics are taught as a curriculum, incorporation in our Christian schools as a curriculum— (Fundamental Marriage Studies), from the Middle to the High schools, would engage students to be abreast of God's standard of marriage—(pre and post-marital counseling course). It should be mentioned here that some higher institutions have marriage and family therapy as a discipline in their curriculum—intending to provide solutions for healing to marriage problems. The question is, why are such institutions interested in providing healing or resolution of marriage problems, rather than educating people on the fundamental biblical and counseling principles of marriage from the initial stages of their lives which could serve as a "preventive measure" for future marriage journeys?

Marriage is the institution that begets the fabric of society, hence the introduction of its fundamental principles to our Christian schools is appropriate, the right thing to do, and then also the strength to the very fabric of society. Moreover, the fundamental biblical and counseling principles of marriage taught before marriage would help to curtail the societal menace of promiscuous lifestyle, deviant behavior, and its effects, as well as rampant divorces. Scriptures attest to "Train up a child in the way he should go, and when he is old, he will not depart from it (Proverbs 22:6). The main goal of this study is how fundamental biblical principles and counseling principles would help solve recurrent marital issues and provide a basis for marriage longevity. Again, the question is, do people go through counseling before their marriage journey— pre and post counseling? If so, do such counseling based on the fundamental biblical principles, human ideologies, or experiences? Scriptures assert that a house whose foundation is not built on (God—Christ teachings) cannot stand the test of time (Matt. 7:24-27), and therefore, its consequences would be disastrous. The Book of Proverbs opine that without counsel, plans go awry, but in the multitude of counselors, they are established (Prov.15:22). Matthew R. Akers likewise opines that "The long-term goal of biblical counseling is to habituate counselees to the practice of finding in Scripture solutions to their inquiries—Scripture is not a book of recommendations, or a work containing valuable "diamond in a dunghill" of inconsistent half-truths. Rather, God's Word is—the supreme standards by which all humans conduct, creeds, and religious opinions should be tried. Counselors can say with assurance, "Thus says the Lord," when they explain what the Bible requires of counselees".[5]

Counseling sessions again, do instruct counselees that Scripture is a God-given, infallible resource. As such, it conveys the proper course of action for any conceivable situation in which believers find themselves (cf. 2Tim.3:16). In this regard, the [fundamental biblical and counseling principles] for potential couples mirror any other type of guidance counselors may provide."[6] Since the fundamental Christian principles of a Christian marriage seem to be broad and comprehensive, the areas of discussion will focus on the following three chapters.

---

[5] Mathew R. Akers, *Equally Yoked, A Premarital Counseling Primer for Multiethnic Christian Couples* (Eugene, Oregon: Wipf and Stock Publishers, 2016), 127.

[6] Akers, *Equally Yoked*, 126.

Chapter one of the study would deliberate on the concept of marriage. In this respect the question such as: what is the meaning of marriage? What is the foundation, purpose, and significance of marriage? will be addressed. The understanding of the concept will help to enlighten potential Christian couples to appreciate and cope with their marriage well. This is necessary because the fundamental reasons that marital vices exist in the community is the *lack of knowledge* of God's Word"[7] and counseling principles which most Christians are woefully unaware as to the foundations for marriage.[8]

Chapter two will discuss the fundamental guiding principles in choosing a lifetime partner. Generally, the reasons that drive people into marriage relationships are varied, therefore the philosophical motivational question would be: what are the wrong and right reasons for marriage and their implications? Is the potential couple psychologically matured, emotionally balanced, socially anchored, economic sound, physically, culturally, and spiritually mature? I used to call this "maturity readiness." These questions are very vital

---

[7] Tokumboh Adeyemo, *Africa Bible Commentary, A One-Volume Commentary Written by 70 Africa Scholars* (Nairobi, Kenyan: Hippo Books, 2006), 1043.

[8] Mohler, R. Albert, God, Marriage, and the Family: Rebuilding the Biblical Foundation' Journal of the Evangelical Theological Society; Lynchburg Vol. 50, Iss. 1, (March 2007): 167-170. Accessed 1/13/20 at Amridge University library

especially towards one's preparedness in choosing a partner in marriage. Moreover, chapter three will discuss the issue of what and how can biblical and counseling principles help in the longevity of a lifetime marriage—the principles of prolonging a Christian marriage. We are very much optimistic that careful study and application of these successive biblical and counseling principles in a marriage relationship would help to-be- Christian-couples understand and appreciate the fundamental basis of marriage and its longevity and then also help to curtail the menace of divorce within our churches and the society at large. According to Barber J. Cyril, the major cause for problems inside or outside of marriage is the violation of biblical principles of effective living and interpersonal relationships.[9]

The sources of materials for this work will be the Christian Scriptures—(Bible), and other secondary scholarly sources. The ensuing discussion deliberate about the concept of Christian marriage.

---

[9] Barber J. Cyril, "Growth Counseling, Pt 1: Enriching Marriage and Family Life" *Journal of Psychology & Theology*, 2 no 4 Fall 1974, p 322-323. ATLA, Accessed 1/9/20), 322.

1

THE CONCEPT OF A CHRISTIAN MARRIAGE

What is marriage

Marriage is an intimate, exclusive, life-long covenant relationship between a man and a woman wherein a new family is established,[10] (gender emphasized). It is the formalization and sanctification of the union of man and woman.[11] Garland discussed various theologian's definition of marriage. She posited that "The Roman Catholic theologians by the twelve-century viewed marriage as a *natural association,* which God had created as the appropriate channel for sexuality and the means for producing and raising children in the service and love of God…marriage was considered a contractual unit, when two parties voluntarily and freely entered (into) for a lifetime of love and service…marriage was identified as a *sacrament.* The

---

[10] Tremper Longman III, *The Baker Illustrated Bible Dictionary,* (Grand Rapids, Michigan: Baker Publishing Group, 2013), 1107.

[11] Douglas, and Tenney, *Zondervan Illustrated Bible Dictionary* 898.

union of body, soul, and mind symbolized the eternal union between Christ and the church, bringing sanctifying grace to the couple, the church, and the community".[12] Regarding the Protestant Reformers, they "Held on to the naturist perspective of marriage as an association created by God for procreation and caregiving. They also kept the contractual perspective, which posits that marriage is a voluntary association entered into by mutual consent. They rejected the view of marriage as a sacrament, however. Marriage for the Reformers was a social institution independent of the church and conferred no sanctifying grace".[13] Lutheran theologians on the other hand stated that "Marriage is the present community for a couple, not a sacramental union for eternal life…If one broke that community – the couple could sue for divorce. And because marriage is a social contract, marriage had to be public, involving parental consent, witnesses, and church consecration and registration. Parents were given a more significant role in the marriage of their children that they had previously had. They had God-given authority to judge the maturity and readiness of the couple for marriage, as well as the legality of

---

[12] Garland, Family Ministry, *A Comprehensive Guide* 73.

[13] Garland, Family Ministry, *A Comprehensive Guide* 77.

their prospective relationship".[14]

The Calvinists theologians were of the view that "Marriage is not a sacrament, but it is more than Luther's social contract. Marriage is a covenant that involves not only the couple but the entire community…marriage includes the couple's parents, two witnesses, the minister, and the magistrate…an institution of the earthly kingdom alone that functioned primarily to keep persons free from sins of lust, fornication, and adultery".[15] On the part of the Anglicans, "They built on the Catholic sacramental model, the Lutheran social model, and the Calvinist covenant model. Marriage is certainly a symbol of Christ's love of the church, as well as both a social contract and a covenant, but more than these, marriage and family symbolize the common good—the good of the couple, their children, the church and the state".[16] Robert W. Weise on the other hand declared that "Marriage is God's divine and blessed walk of life for man and woman being true to each other, to be fruitful, to beget children, and to nurture and bring them up to the glory of God. Marriage is necessary so that men and women can lead a chaste and decent life

---

[14] Garland, Family Ministry, *A Comprehensive Guide* 77.

[15] Garland, Family Ministry, *A Comprehensive Guide* 78.

[16] Garland, Family Ministry, *A Comprehensive Guide* 78.

within the marriage covenant. God's word returns us to the biblical basics of the divine institution of marriage of a man and a woman as the one-flesh union of a husband and wife."[17] Marriage as a social and spiritual institution is the centerpiece of God's design for mankind and has been the primary societal building block from the beginning of history[18] therefore the sanctity and the necessary respect of the enterprise should not be compromised.

The implication of the preceding discussions suggests that marriage is a covenant, a sacred oath between a man and a woman instituted by and publicly entered into before God, and usually consummated by sexual intercourse. It is also a socially recognized universal institution that is found in every society, a social contract of man and woman for the satisfaction of physical, biological, social, psychological, and spiritual needs of the male and female (Gen 2:23 – 25).

---

[17] Robert W. Weise, "Marriage the Divine and Blessed Walk of Life" *Concordia Journal*, 40 no 1Wint 2014, (Accessed on 1/9/2020 at Amridge University library), 46.

[18] Colin Thane, Seager. "A Biblical Foundation Counseling Strategy to Direct Couples to Become One Flesh in Marriage," *Liberty University*, ProQuest Dissertations Publishing, 2014. 3644295.Accessed on 1/12/20 at Amridge University library.

Significance and purpose of marriage

Marriage is important to God and for Christians because it is a precious gift from God (Prov. 18:22; 19:14). It is part of God's plan for creation that men and women should live together and provides a relationship through which husband and wife support each other (Gen. 1:26; 2:18; Eccl. 4:9 – 12), and this relationship is built on selfless love and faithfulness (Heb. 13:4). Its other significances are to circumvent loneliness (Gen. 2:18). *For companionship, intimate relationship, security, and protection* (Eccl. 4:9-12), and *to evade temptation to sin* (1Cor. 7:1-3). Scriptures talk about the purpose of marriage that, 'a man will leave his father and his mother and cleaves to his wife, and they shall become one flesh. And the man and his wife were both naked and were not ashamed', (Gen. 2:24-25). The purpose of the preceding text expresses the unification of the husband and the wife; thus, the man **leaves** his father and mother, **cleaves** to his wife, and be **united** together as **one flesh.** Patton John posited that "It is good for men and women to be committed to one another in a marriage relationship because in such a relationship they not only relieve their loneliness but partially exemplify or illustrate God's commitment to persons and their ultimate value".[19]

---

[19] Patton John, "Pastoral perspective on marriage and family counseling." *The Journal of Pastoral Care* 33, no. 1 (March 1979): 38-43.

Again, "Man was formerly "united" to his parents in a familial relationship, but when he marries, the covenantal relationship with his parents is superseded by the new relationship with his wife. Thus, in establishing the covenantal relationship of marriage, the man and the woman form a new family unit (they become 'one flesh')".[20] The nakedness of both the man and the wife likewise implies their intimate relationship, and more so transparency in their entire life. No secrecy, no hidden agenda, sound mind, (no suspicions), a clear conscience, and total love for each other, and additionally, for procreation and to take total custody of God's creation (Gen. 1:27-28).

The foundation of the institution of marriage

Marriage is an important and crucial institution in the Bible. "Its foundation is established as early as Genesis 1, and Revelation 19:6—10 describes our union with Christ as a great wedding feast. Marriage, after all, unites two human beings in the most intimate and passionate relationship possible… Our relationship with our spouse and our relationship with God are the only two relationships where jealousy may be legitimate".21 Marriage was designed, instituted and initiated

---

[20] Longman, *The Baker Illustrated Bible Dictionary,* 1108.

[21] Joel B. Green, *The Everyday Study Edition*, (Dallas: Word Pub. 1996), 50.

by God. "God highlights the first expressed inadequacy within creation: the man is alone (the need for companionship). The solution to the man's solitude is found not among the animals, but in a creature specifically created to address the problem of his solitude: woman. She is created from his "rib" or "side" so that she is more like him than any of the animals. She is a complement [not supplement] to him. She is described as a "helper suitable for him", which highlights her fulfillment of the inadequacy God had previously identified".22

"Then the LORD God said, "It is not good that the man should be alone; I will make him a helper fit for him" … So, the LORD God caused a deep sleep to fall upon the man, and while he slept took one of his ribs and closed up its place with flesh, and the rib which the LORD God had taken from the man he made into a woman and brought her to the man". The man said, this is now bone of my bones and flesh of flesh; she shall be called 'woman' for she was taken out of man" (Gen 2:18, 21-22). The prior Scripture substantiates the fact that a man and a woman were created for marriage (monogamy), "Therefore a man shall leave his father and mother and be joined to his wife, and they [the man and the woman] shall become one flesh (Gen 2:24)", and not one man and two women (polygamy) or vice-

---

[22] Longman, *The Baker Illustrated Bible Dictionary*, 1107.

versa, two men and one woman (polyandry). It was not man and man, or woman and woman (homosexual); and it was not man/woman and animal (bestiality). And Adam said, "This is now bone of my bones, and flesh of my flesh; She shall be called Woman because she was taken out of Man" (Gen. 2:23, NKJ). The above Scripture suggests the fundamental equality between males and females as well as distinguishing between the two people in terms of individual function. It also gives the impression that their human bodies are similar, but their features as well as their genders are different. The Scriptures also appear to authenticate that both have the same nature, i.e., body, soul and spirit, and in that aspect, love, respect, and dignity, must be accorded to each person. The man is the head and woman helper does not suggest inferiority on the part of the woman but rather order or leadership, an important ingredient in the marriage (newly formed community) to avoid disorder in the marriage institution. When there is a community (more than one person) there must be a leader (head).

Adeyemo likewise asserted that "The word 'helper' does not mean that the woman was to be the man's servant, parent, or keeper. Rather, she was to compliment him. Working alongside him…the woman was not born of the man. She was not the man's child, which would have given him moral authority over her. Rather, God formed her from the man's rib, close to his heart, to establish the intimate link between them in their very creation. The woman will consider the man as part of her very being, and the man will see the woman as the help he needs, without whom he is incomplete. In this way, the man will help his wife to live up to her potential, with thankfulness for God's gift of companionship".[23] Adeyemo again posited that "This ideal union ordained by the Creator cannot exist in a polygamous relationship between a man and several women (polygamy) or between a woman and several men (polyandry). Nor can there be perfect complementarity in a homosexual relationship between two men or between two women. God condemns all sexual relationships that involve anything other than one man and one woman (Rom. 1:27; 1Tim 1:8 – 10 [1Cor.6:9; Lev. 18:22, 20:13])".[24] The next chapter will deliberate on fundamental guiding principles in choosing a lifetime partner.

---

[23] Tokunboh Adeyemo, *Africa Bible Commentary, A One-Volume Commentary Written by 70 Africa Scholars,* (Nairobi: Kenyan, Hippo Books. 2006), 14.

[24] Adeyemo, *Africa Bible Commentary,* 14.

2

THE FUNDAMENTAL GUIDING PRINCIPLES IN CHOOSING A LIFETIME PARTNER

There seem to be several reasons that motivate people into marriage: The following list gives us various **wrong** and **right** motives underlining the basis for "signing up" (entering into) for marriage.

Wrong reasons for marriage:
a) Want to be free from parent(s)'s pressure
b) Just want to have sex with someone (one chosen person) and stop the immoral acts
c) To ease too much loneliness
d) Want to be happy with someone
e) To show others that I am an adult
f) Because of the illicit pregnancy which would show up later and bring some sort of shame
g) Just because he/she loves me and doesn't want to lose him/her.

h) Just want to save, rescue or help someone
i) Because I want to give birth and have babies.
j) He /she has a respectable job and money to take of us
k) All my friends are married, and I am being left behind.
l) Just want to have a wedding and wear the extravagant dress
m) I am getting older and for fear that no one else will want to marry me
n) To have someone to make me a complete person
o) To show that I am also in love with or loved by someone
p) For the sake of immigration purposes
q) I am tired of being single for too long
r) Friends, church members, family members, colleagues at work are pressuring me into getting married
s) I do not want people to gossip about our friendship.
t) To get health or other insurance benefits from my spouse's employer
u) Just want to get someone to cook for me, and take care of the house
v) He is handsome, and she is pretty
w) The person is popular/famous/celebrity and comes from a renowned family or home
x) The person is rich and comes from a rich family
y) The person will shower gifts, money, and everything I want/need

Right reasons for marriage

a) I am in love with him/her and have the desire to share my life and to live a lifetime companionship with him/her

b) I want to feel connected with the person I loved and to grow with that person in all aspects of life, and willingness to be there for one another while we fulfill our own needs and dreams.

c) I am psychologically, emotionally, socially, economically, physically, culturally, and spiritually ready and matured to have my lifetime partner.

The motives behind the wrong reasons are the **conditionalities** that are attached to those views, whereas the right reasons are unconditional. The question to ask is if those conditions cease to exist, will the individual continue to be in the relationship? People should bear in mind that life's conditions are not permanent, therefore marriage should not be based on conditions but rather the premise of **true love** (**agape**) which seems to be the ultimate standard for marriages.

Factors to be considered in preparation towards marriage

Some questions need to be asked when one decides to go into marriage, and I called them Maturity readiness. The questions are as follows:

- Am I **psychologically/mentally matured/fit?** (wife before friends, not a bully, hot-tempered, abusive, or insulting, cursing, egoistic or self-centeredness, etc.,).

- Am I **emotionally balanced?** (sympathetic, empathetic, concern for others, cope with the unexpected/unwanted as in cases of sickness, grief, poverty, job loss, able to comfort, willing to support/help my partner, etc.,).

- Am I **socially anchored?** (respect others and their views, not discriminate, friendly, faithful, speak good of others/vice versa, hospitable, kind person, support the marginalized, able to meet community expectation(s), etc.,)

- Am I **economically sound?** (having a job/working, financially stable, prudent use of money, frugal or not wasting and misusing of resources, not a miser, know about saving money for posterity, ready to take care of my future spouse and children, etc.,)

- Am I **physically matured?** (age-wise, behave and think like an adult, put away childish behavior, have understanding, knowledge in life matters, able to apply wisdom to life issues, healthy/good strength, not sick/weak, not dirty person, not body smell, cleanliness, have intermittent medical checkups, not obese or working to minimize obesity, functional organs in place, exercise to keep your body in shape, etc.,). Being strong physically is paramount to marriage because, one needs the energy to work to take care of him/herself and the family, for childbearing and caring, and any other life responsibilities and pressures that may arise.

- Am I **culturally matured?** (having good manners, courteousness/politeness, not spitting on the floor, well dressed, well behaved in public, respect for the elderly, know how to talk to people, how to greet, laugh in public, how to cook basic food, clean your environment, lay your bed, mopping, washing and ironing of clothes, welcome and serve visitors, etc.,)

- Am I **spiritually matured?** (know the Word, read, study, and apply the Scriptures to situations, holding on to your faith, unmovable in the Lord, having personal devotion, prayer, fasting, going to church, involved in church activities, and supporting the church in her endeavors in kind and finances, learning to and be willing to pray with the potential spouse/children, etc.,).

Choosing a partner when "ready"

Making the choice is a process and not just a one-day affair. Sometimes it takes a brief time, but for others may take some amount of time depending on the individual who is making that step. In all instances, one should be careful not to rush. This is a lifetime decision so the need to exercise patience is very paramount. Adam was very lucky, he had only Eve, so there were no other women to choose from. Most of the cultures in our world today is such that men are the initiators and women are to respond. There are few occasions that one would see a woman proposing to a man, but by and large, men make the proposal and women respond in the affirmative. The following suggestions will give us some *fundamental guiding principles* in making the right choice as to who to marry. Remember, strife to look for compatibility at all **three** dimensions of **spirit, soul,** and **body,** and NOT in the reverse order.

Ask God in prayer

Seek the face of God to direct you to the right one/person. Why God? After all, He has given us our will to make our choices. Yes, but the reason is that God is the initiator of marriage, he made the woman for Adam; he knows the end from the beginning; he is our father and knows what is best and suitable for us out of the numerous candidates around us. The wisest man who ever lived on earth stated that "House and wealth are inherited from fathers, but a **prudent wife** is from the **LORD**", (Prov. 19:14). This same King Solomon further posited that "Unless the Lord builds the house, they labor in vain who build it; Unless the Lord guards the city, the watchmen stays awake in vain", (Psa. 127:1).

King David advised: "Commit your ways to the Lord, trust also in Him, And He shall bring it to pass", (Psa. 37:5). John the apostle additionally alluded to Jesus' assertion, "And whatever you ask in My name, that I will do, that the Father may be glorified in the Son. If you ask anything in My name, I will do it", (John 14:13). Prayer is very necessary because the devil can deceive people for the right choices (Gen. 29:21-25) and misled one through physical appearance **(infatuation)**. The book of Proverbs states that "Charm is deceptive, and beauty is fleeting, but a woman who fears the Lord is to be praised"

(Prov. 31:30). According to **Shakespeare,** "All that glitters is not gold", that is, not everything shiny and superficially attractive is valuable. Beauty will fade whether you like it or not. If you doubt it, look at your parents or inquire from Hollywood for confirmation.

Choose a believer like you and not an unbeliever

It does not please God for a Christian to marry an unbeliever (non-Christian). Do not get conceited to think you can make your spouse become a Christian. That is a deception from the devil. Neither you nor your partner's love can change the spouse. Also, be cautious of those who become overnight "Super Christians" because they want you or your attention to them. God sounded a warning to the Israelites regarding marriages with the heathens, "Nor shall you make marriages with them. You shall not give your daughter to their son, nor take their daughter for your son. For they will turn your sons away from following Me, to serve other gods; so, the anger of the LORD will be aroused against you and destroy you suddenly", (Deut. 7:3-4). You may consult Sampson for advice on this. Again, "Therefore take careful heed to yourselves, that you love the LORD your God. Or else, if indeed you do go back, and cling to the remnant of these nations—these that remain among you—and make marriages with them, and go into them and they to you, know for certain that the LORD your God will no longer drive out these nations from before you. But they shall be **snares** and **traps** to you, and **scourges** on your sides and **thorns** in your eyes, until you perish from this good land which the LORD your God has given you", (Joshua 23:11-13). Paul likewise admonishes believers not to be unequally yoked together with unbelievers. For what fellowship has righteousness with lawlessness? And what communion has light with darkness? And what accord has Christ with Belial? Or what part has a *believer* with an *unbeliever?* (2Cor. 6:14-15). In (Gen. 24), we see the great length Abraham goes to—combined with God's amazing answer to prayer—to ensure that his son Isaac marries believing Rebekah. In (Gen. 27:46 – 28:6), we see Rebekah and Isaac's disgust at the marriage of their son Jacob to marry a Canaanite/Hittite woman. This is not racism, it's God's statue, and it should not be compromised. Total obedience is required of the Christian. **Again:** never entertain the thought that you will marry an unbeliever and change the person after the marriage. It might not work, nor is there a guarantee, you cannot change an unbeliever.

Talk to your Christian parents/guardian/pastor

The purpose is for them to help you in prayer to make the right choice. With the background of their rich experiences and counseling in marriages, they could be a source of guidance. Scripture says, "Where there is no counsel, the people fall; But in the multitude of counselors there is safety", (Prov. 11:14). "Without counsel, plans go awry, but in the multitude of counselors they are established, (Prov. 15:22)".

Suggestion from close individuals

Your parents/guardian/pastor/friend/close relatives or anyone you trust can suggest someone to you, but **do not** let them impose that potential person on you if you are not convinced in your heart and do not have the inner peace and joy of accepting that person. Such instances can sometimes bring hatred, resentment, and animosity in your marriage when troubles begin to surface in the relationship, and the results would be blaming those who chose for you. If such a suggestion comes on your way, have enough time to pray and make sure you are led by the Holy Spirit into that marriage.

Other important factors for consideration

Education – Does he/she have some sort of education? (unanticipated problems will arise for a graduate who marries a fifth-grader)

Work/job – Is he/she working or a potential worker?

Church/fellowship – Does he/she go to the same church with you or have the same faith as far as your Christian beliefs are concerned?

Roots: Does he/she come from your country of origin or probably speak and understand your language? These factors help communicate very well and likewise help to understand your environment and make it easy to relate better in the marriage relationship. If it turns to be the opposite, then bear in mind that sacrifices and adjustments cannot be ruled out as far as keeping the marriage is concerned.

Making the move

The seeker should have this in mind that, he/she is searching for a human being but not an angel, and so should not "dream" as if there are superhumans who would drop from heaven to choose from, but rather, someone within the person's familiar environment. The areas the seeker can look at for the potential partner may be from the church, community, schoolmates, friends, youth groups, work or business places, other religious or social gatherings, hometown, or someone suggested by your family members as the seeker is led by the Holy Spirit. If you find someone, do not rush to propose. Do not also think that someone may overtake you and propose to that person. Marriage is not a race. *The race is not to the swift, nor the battle to the strong... (Eccl. 9:11).* Continue to pray about the person, find a way to befriend, or connect with the person. Study and get to know about the person very well, and find out the person's Christian, and family background. The numerous interactions between both of you, meeting together at some gatherings, knowing each other better as friends through various communication levels, will sum up to build a strong friendship and closeness. When you are fully convinced, well-settled in your heart, you will experience the peace and joy of the Holy Spirit (very strong evidence) that the person you found is the right one. And when you're very optimistic that the potential person seems to be interested in you, then you can go ahead to propose, or accept it, (on the part of the woman).

What if it does not work

If the potential person says, no, or wait, please do not rush into hasty conclusions like feeling insignificant, worthless, inferior, etc. Marriage is a lifetime journey, once entered you cannot turn back, so take time to continue in prayer and still be friends. Perhaps the partner needs time to make a decision or even prepare and to be ready for the marriage journey. From experience, sometimes a NO answer is a blessing in disguise. That "NO" might be saving you from a lifetime of misery. If at a point in time, let's say, three or more months to a year passed by and there is no positive response from the potential person, I would suggest you leave the person and search again for another person through the same process as mentioned earlier. It is normal to be disappointed when the unfortunate ("NO" answer) happens, though a lot of resources may have been spent, and leaving the person may seem difficult. There is nothing wrong to give a gift to someone you wanted to marry, but the gifts are not a license for one to accept your proposal. Potential people seeking for a spouse should not use flamboyant gifts or money to entice the opposite sex nor as a motivational factor to win the person. This would have some negative effects on the marriage life if the potential person accepted you based on those goodies. The question is if even you got married and the goodies are not forthcoming due to lack of resources, what would be the state of the marriage affair? So, if goodies and money have been spent, the giver should let it go with no animosity for the sake of peace.

If both agree

There is no joy than a potential person saying **"yes"** after the proposal. This is also the time the temptation begins if extra caution, especially for believers is not taken. The temptations to kissing, carousing, touching both sensitive parts of the body, and arousing sexual desire or even having sex are strongest. That is why Paul admonished believers and to-be-couples to exercise restraint of their sexual desires. "It is God's will that you should be sanctified: that you should avoid sexual immorality; that each of you should learn to control your own body in a way that is holy and honorable, not in passionate lust like the pagans, who do not know God; and that in this matter no one should wrong or take advantage of a brother or sister. The Lord will punish all those who commit such sins, as we told you and warned you before. God did not call us to be impure but to live a holy life. Therefore, anyone who rejects this instruction does not reject a human being but God, the very God who gives you his Holy Spirit, (1Thes. 4:3—8)." Paul admonished believers to "Flee from sexual immorality. All other sins a person commits are outside the body, but whoever sins sexually, sins against their own body. Do you not know that your bodies are temples of the Holy Spirit, who is in you, whom you have received from God? You are not your own; you were bought at a price. Therefore, honor God with your bodies (1Cor 6:18-20)". As a believer, you do not have the right to do any lustful things that will lead to committing sexual sin. You have not yet married, this is just the beginning of a lifetime journey, therefore the need to exercise restraint is imperative, and more so to resist the enemy from having a hand in the marriage. (Heb 13:4), TRUE LOVE WAITS (TLW).

What to do next (Get Married)

Consult both parents about your decision and for their approval, and more so your pastor(s) for the necessary counseling process and make the necessary preparation for your marriage. Both families are very vital in the marriage process because marriage is not an individual affair. The family support and the pronouncement of blessings are very vital to both to-be-couple. Adam's and Eve's parents (God) pronounced his blessings on them … And God blessed them, and God said to them, "Be fruitful and multiply, and fill the earth and subdue it; and have dominion over the fish of the sea and the birds of the air and over every living thing that moves upon the earth, (Gen. 1:27-28)". The family of Rebekah likewise pronounced their blessings on her, "And they blessed Rebekah and said to her, "Our sister, may you increase to thousands; may your offspring possess the cities of their enemies (Gen 24:60)". Isaac pronounced blessings on Jacob (Gen. 28:1—4). To-be-couples should not lose sight of this important aspect of spiritual blessings as far as the marriage journey is concerned. Since both people are prepared and ready for marriage, there is no need or use for the contemporary phrase "WE ARE COURTING OR DATING". Make the necessary plans with both families, and the church for the traditional marriage, and the wedding as well, depending upon what both of you, your families, and the church accept and recognize. When the set time comes, go ahead, marry, and get together in peace with the blessings of both families, and God. Someone asked a pastor a question thus, "Is it right for both potential couples to engage in sex to test themselves before marriage"? The person continued, "Because when one wants to buy clothing, the person should put it on to see if it fits or test-drive a car before making payment". The pastor's response was that: human beings are not material things such as clothing and cars but rather persons created in the image of God. Moreover, marriage is not seeing before believing, but rather the opposite—believing (trusting) before seeing. It is not food or cookies where one would taste before buying, but as an analogy (although not in magnitude if I may be permitted) to service, once rendered or provided it cannot be undone. Would you say to your doctor after he/she has attended to you "undo or take back your service?" Christian marriage is the original pattern of marriage and does not follow a worldly style of dating or courting where individuals stay together and get themselves in sexual intercourse or "testing the waters" (sex) before getting into it. Marriage is holy matrimony ordained by God for mutual and sacred intimacy between a man and a woman for a lifetime relationship. ONLY IN THE INSTITUTION OF MARRIAGE IS SEXUAL INTERCOURSE ALLOWED. And there are good and strong reasons why God set that boundary. Something which has been instituted and ordained by God should not be abused but accorded with respect and dignity. God is the initiator of marriage and he blessed it for Adam and Eve before consummation took place (Gen. 1:27-27), likewise for Rebekah and Isaac (Gen. 24:60). We also read from Scripture that Joseph did not touch Mary until she had borne Jesus (Matt.1:18, 25; Luke 1:34).

The principle is this, marriage first then consummation—(with sexual intercourse) follows. Scriptures have emphasized that any sexual activities engaged in before marriage and outside the borders of marriage is sin, and the culprits will be judge by God according to their actions (Heb 13:4). If you are not ready for marriage wait till your time comes. King Solomon admonition "I charge you, o daughters of Jerusalem, by the gazelles or by the does of the field, do not stir up nor awaken love until it pleases" (Song of Solomon 3:5). The text implies that if you are not ready for marriage avoid sexual provocation. The next chapter discusses the principles of Christian marriage longevity.

3

THE PRINCIPLES OF A CHRISTIAN MARRIAGE LONGEVITY

Reasons that Contributes to Rampant Divorces

There are several reasons which seem to be contributing to rampant divorces which negate Christian marriage longevity. Some of these reasons are immoral issues, such as promiscuous life of partner(s) as evident in adultery, fornication, homosexuality, and the like; laziness, unemployment or loss of job leading to poverty or bankruptcy, which renders partners inept to take care of the family, etc. Diana R. Garland submitted that "An examination of divorce statistics, for example, reveals that divorce rates are much higher among the poor and the unemployed. Poverty and economic uncertainty are usually out of the control of the spouses, yet they create conditions that make marital survival more difficult."[25]

Other issues that surfaced on a random sampling conducted in a church setting and some experience from the

---

[25] Diana R. Garland, *Family Ministry*, 172-173.

writers pastoral counseling on the various reasons for divorce are: sicknesses (chronic, incurable or stigmatized like leprosy, HIV); lack of sexual satisfaction – (demand for too much sex from a partner, lack of libido, not achieving orgasm, erectile dysfunction, etc.); infertility; alleged superstition of a partner being a witch/wizard, pressure from extended family for a partner to marry a second wife or the need for a male child to inherit family property due to family traditional values; lack of formal education on the part of the woman when the man's social status is elevated; lack of transparency; jealousy, self-centeredness; immigration problems, etc. No wonder some Pharisees came to test Jesus whether it was lawful for a man to divorce his wife for any and every reason (Matt. 19: 3 – 8).

In a church group discussion on "Why do people get divorced?" Bissett Don recounted that "There is a complex interdigitation of cultural and personal variables that contribute to the divorces… the number one cause of divorce reported by participants in the group was infidelity. The pursuit of sexual experience and pleasure, the de-sanctification of sexuality in marriage, and the liberalization of previously more rigid sexual mores; the economic independence that [women] achieved, due, in part, to the changes in our society. Many of the women often felt 'locked in' by past financial constraints.

When their financial abilities enabled them to do so, they sought to free themselves of a relationship they had previously felt constrained to maintain".[26]

Don made mention that "The way the law has changed to make it easier for people to become divorced [$399.00 "No spouse's signature required"]. The whole arena of high expectations in our society surrounding marital relationships. We are living in a narcissistic age in which immediate gratification is valued over long-term investment. An individual reward is frequently preferred over the marital relationship. Adaptability, mobility, and replacement are sometimes praised over perseverance and loyalty. The assumption that one is owed emotional fulfillment and self-realization through marriage and personal happiness from the marital partner is at the heart of narcissistic conception."[27]

Moreover, [people] have been "dumped" because they were unable to satisfy the high expectations of emotional and sexual fulfillment and a continuing, romantic love in providing a pathway to self-realization for their partners; and gender differences—women most often complain that men are

---

[26] Bissett, Don. "A Church-Sponsored Divorce Recovery Through Group Experience'. *Journal of Family Ministry* 4, no. 2 (1990): 45-53.

[27] Don. *"A Church-Sponsored Divorce Recovery Through Group Experience."* 45-53.

insensitive, do not know how to express their deepest emotions, and are inept at cultivating emotional intimacy. Some of the women demanding emotional fulfillment find these men handicapped and move on to other relationships,[28] and the consequences thereof seem to have some negative effects on couples who have been separated as such: humiliation, family separation, animosity, grief, cantankerousness, depression, sickness, truancy in children, even suicidal attempts, death, etc. These consequences disastrously affect the church, and society, hence the motivation to study some of these biblical and guiding principles to curb some of these divorce menaces and help in maintaining the longevity of the marital journey.

The following guiding principles have been provided to offer potential couples some guidance in helping marriage longevity. These are oneness; transparency; adaptability; love/humility; couples' responsibilities towards their family; faithfulness/fidelity in sexual intimacy; the couple's role; forgiveness; and the family's spirituality. The subsequent deliberations will focus on the issues listed above.

---

[28] Don. *"A Church-Sponsored Divorce Recovery Through Group Experience."* 45-53.

Oneness in Christian Marriage

The Oxford Living Dictionary defines oneness as "The fact or state of being unified or whole, though comprised of two or more parts, or the state of being in harmony with someone or something".[29] When the meaning of oneness is applied in the marriage scenario, it describes the biblical idea of husband and wife becoming one, "So they are no longer two but one…" (Matt. 19:6). The question is why oneness is so important in the longevity of marriage? The significance of oneness is realized in God's very nature—the Trinity. An example is seen in the creation of the universe, and humanity (Gen. 1:1 – 3; 26-27); the holistic life of Jesus—his birth (Luke 1:35), baptism (Matt 3:16 – 17), temptation and ministry (Luke 4:1, 14 – 19), and death and resurrection (Rom 8:11). Jesus similarly underscored oneness in his high priestly—prayer recorded in John 17.

Again, oneness bestows God's blessings on his people (Psa.133). Amos stated that "Can two walk together unless they have agreed to do so? (3:3)". The Godhead is one (one unit) and *he* expects married couples created in his image to be one. Garland declared that "Jesus' only lengthy discussion of the subject [marriage] is precipitated by a test question from

---

[29] Oxford Living Dictionary.

the Pharisees about the grounds for divorce (Mt. 19:3 – 12; Mk. 10:2 – 12). He combines texts from Genesis 1:27, 2:24, and 5:2, arguing that marriage has its basis in God's act of creation. He asserted that God has joined the two together, and therefore the bond should not be broken".[30] Oneness helps in companionship, strengthens the weak, provides security and protection (Eccl.4:9-12). The inference from the discourse suggests that married couples need to be one in all spheres of life, thus physically, spiritually, emotionally, financially, planning for family and future dreams, sharing of successes and failures, and all life endeavors. These are processes and therefore require time but focusing to implement them will help to prolong a lifetime marriage.

Transparency in Christian Marriage

Transparency in the context of this study simply means crystal clear in every endeavor of both couples. "…And the man and his wife were both naked and were not ashamed", (Gen. 2:24-25). There should not be any secrecy or hidden agenda, but rather an openness in the marriage. For example, the occupation/job both are doing should be plain and made known to each other, time each goes to work and closes,

---

[30] Garland, *Family Ministry, A Comprehensive Guide*, 169.

paycheck or (income), and any other aspect that relates to the marriage. In Jesus' own words to his disciples, he made mention that "...for all things that I heard from My Father I have made known to you (John 15:15)". The writer of Hebrews describes how all things are naked and open to God, "And there is no creature hidden from His sight, but all things *are* naked and open to the eyes of Him to whom we *must* give account (Heb. 4:13)".

Transparency is so important to Paul's work with the Corinthians. It appears Paul's integrity had been questioned, he knew that because of his history of transparency with the Church of Corinth, they would continue to trust him. Paul stated that "But we have renounced the hidden things of shame, not walking in craftiness nor handling the word of God deceitfully, but by the manifestation of the truth commending ourselves to every man's conscience in the sight of God, (2 Cor. 4:2). O Corinthians! We have spoken openly to you; our heart is wide open (2Cor. 6:11)". Are we making de¬cisions in secret as a way of avoiding accountability or hiding what others would object to? To prolong marriages, couples need to be transparent enough so that both would have a reason and a cause to **trust** themselves.

Adaptability in Christian Marriage

Adaptability means adjusting or becoming used to a new situation for achieving a desired need or outcome, thus in this case accommodating one's spouse. The reason for adaptability is that both couples have different family, cultural, social, economic, or educational backgrounds. What has brought them together is the love and the desire to share their lives, and to live a lifetime companionship. Both feel connected in love, to grow together in all aspects of life, and the willingness to be there for one another while both fulfill their own needs and dreams. Therefore, lack of resilience and adjustment especially when challenges arise, may disintegrate the marriage.

Alluding from the example of David and Michal, daughter of Saul (2 Sam. 6:16, 20 -23), it appears Michal despised David in her heart, which implied she hated, reviled, shunned, rejected and scorned him (David) because of his nakedness when David danced before the Lord when returning the Lord's Ark. Apart from the biblical context or interpretation of the text, Michal was a princess (daughter of King Saul), and it is obvious that she had some royal training, etiquette and nurturing in the palace of her father's kingdom in her upbringing such as in dancing, eating, talking, dressing, etc. David's' background was shepherding, living with flocks in the desert and through God's providential circumstances became a king. Probably he did not have the opportunity to go through such protocol to meet Michal royal standards of training, hence her animosity against David. This insolence caused her something valuable; she went down in the history of Israel as probably the only documented princess who was barren. Tenney and Douglas postulated that "Michal believed that a king should be strong and dignified, and so she was disgusted by David's dancing *as any vulgar fellow would* in front of everyone"[31] and could not adjust to David's actions. "Though Michal truly loved David, she could not comprehend him, and so scoffed at him for rejoicing before the Lord (2 Sam. 6:16—23). As a result, she never had a child."[32] For longevity of a lifetime nuptial relationship, one must do away with pride and make every effort to adjust to each other irrespective of one's varied background.

Serving in Christian Marriage

Serving is a major activity that seems to prolong a lifetime marriage. It involves sacrificing time, energy, finance, and material resources for the interest of one's partner. In some

---

[31] Adeyemo, *Africa Bible Commentary, A One-Volume Commentary Written by 70 Africa Scholars*, 387.

[32] Tenney and Douglas, *Zondervan Illustrated Bible Dictionary*, 941

African cultures, it is demeaning for a husband to cook, help with house chores, bathe children, do the laundry, etc. Such chores, by culture, are meant for the women, and the men likewise as breadwinners for the family. The book of Mark posited that "For even the Son of Man did not come to be served, but to serve, and to give his life as a ransom for many." (Mark 10:42 - 45). DeSilva stated that "In the world greatness is preeminence, power, and recognition. It includes being honored and being served by others. In God's sight greatness consist of serving others and pouring oneself out for them, even as Jesus himself came "not to be served but to serve and give his life as a ransom for many."[33] Marshal succumbed that "Entry into the Kingdom is an entry into the realm of service for God."[34] Christians are expected to serve one another and those in need. Jesus admonished his disciples to serve one another when he washed their feet in (John 14), the task or service which were reserved for the servants or slaves in a household. But he demonstrates this service to show them an example for them to emulate.

---

[33] David A. DeSilva, *An Introduction to the New Testament, Context, Methods & Ministry Formation*, (Downers Grove, Illinois: InterVarsity Press, 2004), 206.

[34] Howard I. Marshall, *New Testament Theology, Many Witnesses, One Gospel*, (Downers Grove, Illinois: Intervarsity Press, 2004), 110.

Service appears to be Jesus' central mission, (Matt 23:12; Mark 10:43 – 44), no wonder he acquired the status of greatness as posited by Paul in (Philippians 2:5 – 11). Peter in his first letter urges believers to love and serve one another as Christ gave them an example (1Peter 4:7 – 11). The implications of the study advocate that serving should not be relegated to the wife alone as some cultures endorse, but rather it should be shared responsibility for both couples for the sake of marriage longevity.

Love and Submission in Christian Marriage

Love seems to be the glue that binds the marriage together. Jesus is love. Jesus demonstrated and expressed his love by giving himself for humanity; he sacrificed his status as God for the sake of people; demonstrated care and kindness, helped everyone, especially the marginalized; healed diseases and broken-hearted, forgave sins, and lastly dying to save those that believe (Isa. 53:3 – 5; Rom. 5:8; 1Pt. 5:25). Paul admonished husbands, to love their wives, just as Christ also loved the church and gave Himself for her, and likewise wives to submit to their husbands (Eph. 5:23-25). Keener made some assertions that,

Most ancient writers expected wives to obey their

husbands, desiring in them a quiet and meek demeanor... Paul differs from the usual conventions, which normally addressed only the male head of the household. The closest Paul comes to specifically define submission here is "respect" (v.33), and in the Greek text, wifely submission to a husband (v. 22) is only one example of general mutual submission of Christians... Although it was assumed that husbands should love their wives, ancient household codes typically told husbands not how to love their wives but how to rule them. Although Paul upholds the ancient ideal of wifely submission, he qualifies it by placing it in the context of mutual submission: husbands are to love their wives as Christ loved the *church, by willingly laying down their lives for them...Both husbands and wives must submit and love (5:2, 21).[35]

This is a reciprocal duty for both couples. Jesus' humility was expressed even at his birth, a King being born in a manger; washing the disciples' feet, a work supposed to be done by slaves; disgraced and humiliated in public, beaten and finally

---

[35] Craig S. Keener, *The Gospel of Matthew: A Socio-Rhetorical Commentary*, (Grand Rapids, Michigan: Wm. B. Eerdmans publishing, 1999), 552.

crucified on the cross: the most excruciating (derived from the word "cross") and shameful at the time. Would couples emulate Jesus' kind of love and humility for their spouses? No attribute of God is more fundamental than God's love. Jesus taught us that our relationships with one another are to reflect that love (Jn. 4:16 – 21).[36] To prolong a lifetime relationship Jesus' standard of love *(agape)* and humility should be imitated. By the way, is it not what you promised to do when you recited your vows? It will be encouraging and uplifting to revisit your marriage vows now and then.

The couple's role *(Submission and Love)* further elaborated by Paul in his letter to the Ephesians, he stated that: *Wives submit to your own husbands, as to the Lord. For the husband is head of the wife, as also Christ is head of the church; and He is the Savior of the body. Therefore, just as the church is subject to Christ, so let the wives be to their own husbands in everything. Husbands, love your wives, just as Christ also loved the church and gave Himself for her, that He might sanctify and cleanse her with the washing of water by the word, that He might present her to Himself a glorious church, not having spot or wrinkle or any such thing, but that she should be holy and without blemish. So, husbands ought to love their own wives as*

---

[36] Garland, *Family Ministry, A Comprehensive Guide*, 209.

their own bodies; he who loves his wife loves himself (Ephesians. 5:22—28).

Wives submit to your own husbands: It seems when some women hear the word submit or submission the question that usually comes to mind is: Are you kidding me? Do you want me to be my husband's slave? Do you want me to do everything he tells me to do and bow to him? Being a submissive wife does NOT mean that you are your husband's slave. The Greek word *(**Hupotassō**)* translated in English as "submit," Paul uses this word here as a military term meaning to "put oneself in rank under another" (thus, yield to one's admonition; be under obedience (obedient); be subject to the authority or one above you; humble). God has ordained the principle of authority and submission in several different spheres:

- Citizens are to be subject to civil authorities (Rom. 13:1; Titus 3:1).
- Slaves are submissive to their masters (Col. 3:22; Titus 2:9).
- Church members to their leaders (1Cor 16:16; Titus 2:15; Heb. 13:17).
- Children to their parents (Eph. 6:1—3; Col. 3:20).
- Wives to their husbands (Eph. 5:22, 24; Titus 2:5; 1Pet. 3:1).

Every time the New Testament speaks to the role of wives, the command is the same: "Be subject to your husband." This does not also mean the wife is inferior to the husband. The whole concept of submission is about subject to order or line of authority in the house. The bottom line is *humility*. The submission of wives to their own husband "phrase" has been emphasized in Scriptures, which implied that God is more particular on that command"

- Wives, submit to your own husbands, as to the Lord (Eph. 5:22)
- Therefore, just as the church is subject to Christ, so let the wives be to their own husbands in **everything** (Eph 5:24).
- For the husband is head of the wife, as also Christ is head of the church (Eph. 5:23)
- Wives, submit to your own husbands, as is fitting in the Lord (Col. 3:18)
- Wives, likewise, *be* submissive to your own husbands (1Pt 3:1)

Submission of wives to their own husband must be demonstrated in:

- **Speech:** Let no corrupt word proceed out of your mouth, but what is good for necessary edification that it may impart grace to the hearers… (Eph 4:29 – 32).

A soft answer turns away wrath, but a harsh word stirs up anger (Prov. 15:1).

- **Conduct:** Wives, likewise, *be* submissive to your own husbands, that even if some do not obey the word, they, without a word, maybe won by the conduct of their wives, when they observe your chaste conduct *accompanied* by fear. (1Pet. 3:1-2).
- **Obedience:** That they admonish the young women to love their husbands, to love their children, to be discreet, chaste, homemakers, good, obedient to their own husbands, that the word of God may not be blasphemed (Titus 2:5). ... being submissive to their own husbands, as **Sarah obeyed Abraham,** calling him **lord**... (1Pet. 3:5-6)
- **Respect:** ...and let the wife see that she respects her husband (Eph. 5:33). Michal despised David and could not give birth (2Sam. 6:16).
- **Service:** Rebekah served the servant of Abraham and his entourage and had a good marriage (Gen. 24:17-21ff).

Submission of Christian wives is very paramount to God, therefore married women should not compromise, but should heed to that Scriptural admonition for a successful lifetime nuptial union. To submit to your own husband does not warrant wives to succumb to their husband's evil and immoral practices that call for God's wrath, (1Cor. 6:9-10), because God would punish couples that engaged in evil.

Husbands love your wives: The Greek word *(Agape "love")* means selfless love or unconditional love, sacrificial love. This love is most frequently used for the **love for God,** the **love for spouses**, and the **love for enemies.** Agape love means action. It means that we act in a loving way towards others. It means we use our mind and our might for the benefit of another, without regard for ourselves. This is the kind of love Jesus demonstrated to us. Scriptures have emphasized that husbands should love their wives:

- Husbands love your wives, just as Christ also loved the church and gave Himself for her (Eph. 5:25).
- So, husbands ought to love their own wives as their own bodies; he who loves his wife loves himself (Eph 5:28)
- Nevertheless, let each one of you so love his own wife as himself (Eph 5:33)
- Husbands, love your wives and do not be bitter toward them (Col 3:19)
- Live joyfully with the wife whom you love all the days of your vain life which He has given you under the sun, all your days of vanity; for that is your portion in life, and in the labor which you perform under the sun (Eccl. 9:9).

Husbands loving their wives must be demonstrated

- **In sacrificial love, giving and providing her needs:** of their time, energy, financial resources (John 3:16). But if anyone does not provide for his own, and especially for those of his household, he has denied the faith and is worse than an unbeliever (1Tim. 5:8).

- **Physical love:** Value her above all other women. Tell your wife she is beautiful, the apple of my eye, *"me do wiase"*— (the one and only lover). Give her words that will make her melt. My beloved spoke and said to me: Rise up, my love, my fair one, and come away (Song of Solomon 2:10).

- **Emotional love:** Let the husband render to his wife the affection due her, and likewise also the wife to her husband. The wife does not have authority over her own body, but the husband *does*. And likewise, the husband does not have authority over his own body, but the wife *does*. Do not deprive one another except with consent for a time (1Cor 7:3).

- **Relational love:** Develop love towards her relatives, children, family members, her job, aspirations, her progress, etc.

- **Genuine love:** In her failures show love, when she is discouraged due to life pressures support her, comfort her, and let her feel she has a husband by her side.

- **Spiritual love:** This geared towards her salvation and her Christian faith. Show her godly love. Teach her the Word of God, pray with her, forgiving one another, have devotion together, lead a holy life, engage her in church activities, and build her up in the things of God. (Joshua 24:15) … "But as for me and my house, we will serve the LORD."

Couple Responsibilities towards their Family

Scriptures encouraged Christian couples to take care of their immediate family. Paul told Timothy to teach the inevitability of taking diligent care of believer's immediate families. "But if anyone does not provide for his own, and especially for those of his household, he has denied the faith and is worse than an unbeliever (1Tim. 5:8)". This calls for the responsibility of both couples to engage in work to take care of themselves and their families (2Thess. 3:10 – 12). The immediate families appear to be the couple's children and their parents. Parents are channels through which both couples came to this world and nurtured to become responsible adults, and therefore, the principle of reciprocity is inevitable until their demise. Keener posited that "Many Jewish teachers regarded the commandment to honor father and mother as the most important in the law. Jewish interpreters included in this commandment providing for [the physical needs of] one's parents when they were old".37

Moreover, Scriptures recapped that children are a heritage from the Lord, the fruit of the womb is a reward according to (Psalm 127:3). Proverbs likewise professed that we should "Train up a child in the way he should go, and when he is old, he will not depart from it (22:6)." Both passages suggest parental responsibilities towards the mandatory assignment of nurturing children according to God's way. They are God's property; therefore, proper training of children would help them throughout their lives. Since both couple's immediate families are important, their holistic support cannot be compromised. Absence and relinquishment of such welfare to the immediate family would have a negative consequence on the sustainability of the marriage. The couple's especially the father supposed to be the king/leader/head and exemplar in the home (Psalm 78:5-8; Eph. 5:25-37; 1Pet. 5:3-4); a provider/investor to the family (Gen. 26:12-16; Eccl.11:1-2; 1Tim. 5:8); a prophet/teacher for the family (Gen. 18:19; Deut. 6:1-9; Prov.

---

37 Keener, *The Gospel of Matthew: A Socio-Rhetorical Commentary*,145.

4:1-4); a loving and disciplinarian father (Prov. 3:11-12; 4:1-9; Eph. 6:4); and a priest/intercessor to the family (Job 1:4-5; 1Sam. 12:23; Rom 8:34). The other role especially the wife is to complement the husband's effort, by practically supervise and nurture the children to attain their God-given potentials (Prov 31; 2Tim. 1:5; Titus 2:4-5).

Fidelity in Christian Marriage

Scriptures ascribed faithfulness as an attribute of God. According to Longman, "Faithfulness is a part of his very being. In the Torah the Israelites are reminded, "The Lord your God is God; he is the faithful God, keeping his covenant of love to a thousand generations of those who love him and keep his commandments" (Deut. 7:9) …Hosea calls God "the faithful Holy One" (Hos. 11:12). Isaiah likewise presents faithfulness as an attribute of God (Isa. 49:7). The people can be assured, for God is unchanging and reliable… Yahweh is ascribed divine honor by his people recognizing and acknowledging his faithfulness and trustworthiness and responding to it in obedience as the people of God".38 "Marriage begins when two people make the clear, unqualified promise to be faithful, each to the other, until the end of their days. That spoken

---

[38] Longman, *The Baker Illustrated Bible Dictionary*, 564.

promise makes the difference… A promise made, a promise witnessed, a promise heard, remembered, and trusted – this is the groundwork of marriage".[39] Faithfulness/fidelity in the marriage relationship is an obligation for both couples, especially when it comes to matters of sexual intimacy. Both have made a vow in the presence of God, his holy angels and witnesses present that they will live together in the holy estate of marriage, to love, comfort, honor, and to keep each other in sickness and in health, forsaking all others so long as both shall live. Paul cautioned that "Let the husband render to his wife the affection due her, and likewise also the wife to her husband. The wife does not have authority over her own body, but the husband *does*. And likewise, the husband does not have authority over his own body, but the wife *does*. Do not deprive one another except with consent for a time… (1Cor. 7:3 – 5)".

The writer of Hebrews also recounted the consequences regarding desecration of the married bed, "Marriage is honorable among all, and the bed undefiled; but fornicators [sexual intercourse between the unmarried] and adulterers [sexual intercourse with someone other than your spouse] God will judge (Heb. 13:4). "'Let marriage be held in honor." "By all" probably means "in all circumstances." … "The marriage

---

[39] Garland, *Family Ministry, A Comprehensive Guide*, 221.

bed" is a euphemism for sexual intercourse".[40] 'Any sexual relationship outside of marriage is immoral and abhorrent to God. All…married couples should learn to understand God's will and purpose for marriage and should preserve his gifts of sexual integrity within the marriage relationship. Marriage is a divine institution that requires believers to take heed of divine advice (Gen. 2:7, 18, 20b-23; Mal. 2:15; Eph. 5:21-33). Purity, integrity, loyalty, and love are the walls that protect this godly institution against sexual sins".[41]

The New Testament contends that sexual intercourse can be properly expressed only in a lifelong marriage. Sexual encounters should honor one another's personhood and needs. Paul rejects casual sexual encounters because a sexual encounter can never be casual (1 Cor. 6). Sex is not just joining of bodies but involves the deepest recesses of the soul (Prov. 6:32; Mt. 15:19; Mk. 7:21). Sex is not to be self-centered so that the spouse becomes an object for self-gratification… The sexual relationship between a man and a woman is undeniably a means for sharing in God's work of creation, but the pleasure

---

[40] Kenneth L. Barker, *The Expositor's Bible Commentary, Abridged Edition, New Testament*, (Grand Rapids, Michigan: Zondervan,: 1994), 1009.

[41] Adeyemo, *Africa Bible Commentary*, 1533.

dimension is part of creation too, and to be celebrated.42 Moreover, the importance of husbands being considerate towards their wives cannot be overemphasized as posited by the apostle Peter, "Husbands, likewise, dwell with them with understanding, giving honor to the wife, as to the weaker vessel, and as being heirs together of the grace of life, that your prayers may not be hindered (1Pt. 3:7)". Faithfulness/fidelity should embody the very core of the [marriage] covenant relationship,43 therefore, couples should close their eyes and ears to the outside "noise" and avoid giving in to old lifestyle as far as keeping the marriage vows is concerned, and in that way, the sustainability of a lifelong bond can be realized.

Communication in Christian Marriage

Communication is a unique tool for the success and sustainability of a lifetime relationship. In a marriage setting, for example, communication is the interaction or dissemination of information or a conversation between couples. It is seen in everyday life and the home. The question is how do people communicate? Communication is done through word, speech, works/activities or deeds, and actions and gestures (body

---

[42] Garland, *Family Ministry, A Comprehensive Guide*, 173.

[43] Longman, *The Baker Illustrated Bible Dictionary*, 565.

language). These are basic forms of communication. It should be such that both couples get the needed understanding of what information they are giving. Is the mode of communication gentle, harsh, rebuking, upsetting, agitating, or confrontational? Paul advised believers that they should, "Let your speech always be with grace, seasoned with salt, that you may know how you ought to answer each one (Col. 4:6 NKJV)". But I say to you that for every idle word's men may speak, they will give an account of it in the day of judgment. For by your words you will be justified, and by your words, you will be condemned (Matt. 12:36-37 NKJV). Again, he also stated that "Let no corrupt word proceed out of your mouth, but what is good for necessary edification that it may impart grace to the hearers… (Eph 4:29 – 32)". The nuance of the discourse suggests that both couples should be courteous in their communication. Not being courteous in communication can result in hard feelings towards one another. Cutting people off when talking, not saying "thank you" "excuse me" and "please," personally attacking one another and being condescending are all examples of poor manners and interpersonal communication that can result in a poor relationship, therefore both couples are to be flexible and kind when interacting with each other. Green pointed that, "When we communicate, we share ideas, thoughts, and feelings with others.

Each act of communication can never be an isolated event, for the means of communication and the understanding of a meaning we give to those words, which actions or expressions we use to express ourselves, and what key events and their significance we allude to are all part of the complex process of communication",[44] therefore any actions or forms of communication must be Christ-centered as far as lifetime nuptial is concerned.

Forgiveness in Christian Marriage

Moreover, one of the essential aspects of a couple's spirituality is the ability to forgive one another. Joel S. Williams in his lecture notes on *guilt and forgiveness in ministry and pastoral counseling* submitted that,

> Forgiveness involves a change in thinking about the offender. Forgiveness removes the burden from our soul; not making any more demands of self; giving up what we consider our rights; a decision, an act of one's own'. Forgiveness improves one's life and health and brings freedom. Forgiveness doesn't change the past…

---

[44] Green, *Holy Bible, Everyday Study Edition*, 1499

but does change the power of the past to control one's present and future, it prevents one from becoming more bitter and ties one to the Spirit of Christ. It's a test case for love, and it goes beyond the ordinally. To be godlike, one needs to forgive (Matt. 5:44 – 45), since life is reciprocal believers [couples] are mandated to forgive (Matt. 5:7; 6: 14 – 15), and in return receives God's blessing.45

The importance of forgiveness as a spiritual entity in a marriage relationship as well as for a believer's life journey cannot be overemphasized. Scriptures likewise attest to that "In him, we have redemption through his blood, the forgiveness of our trespasses, according to the riches of his grace that he lavished on us (Eph.1:7-8, Col. 1:13 - 14)". Forgiveness is a characteristic of God, through his Son Jesus Christ, therefore Christian couples are to imitate this Christlike character for a lifetime sustainable relationship.

The Couples Christian Spirituality

For a lifetime marriage relationship, God should be the center of affairs. King Solomon professed that "Unless the Lord builds the house, they labor in vain who builds it…'

---

[45] Joel S. Williams, "Ministry to Families and Individuals, lecture notes on Guilt and Forgiveness in Ministry and Pastoral Counseling" (Amridge University, 5/29/2020).

(Psa. 127:1)". John likewise alluded to the words of Christ, "…for without Me, you can do nothing (John 15:5)". Garland additionally declared that,

> Unless the Lord builds the house, those who build and labor in vain (Ps.127:1), might well be applied also to the house and home of the marital couple. We can busy around working as hard as we like at our marriage, but labor alone will not ensure success… the belief that a good marriage can be achieved by hard work ignores the imperfection of persons, who can only rely on God's grace to lift them out of their unsuccessful attempts to perfect themselves and their relationships. No matter how hard spouses try, the maintenance of the marriage covenant cannot be guaranteed by their hard work. Flawed people cannot form a perfect relationship. A strong and satisfying relationship is not something persons can assure, but it is the fruit that comes in the process of relating to one another by the grace of God.46

Reflections of the study propose that the couple's spirituality has to do with their dependence and relationship with God. Their readiness to spiritual discipline such as,

---

[46] Garland, *Family Ministry, A Comprehensive Guide* 171-172.

knowing the Word, reading, studying, meditating, and applying Scripture to life situations, holding on to their Christian faith, unmovable in the Lord, having personal devotions, learning to and be willing to pray and fast together, forgiving themselves, attending church together, involving in church activities, supporting the church in her endeavors in kind and finances, and sharing their faith to others, especially unbelievers. Such an act of spiritual outworking will help couples to grow spiritually and likewise endure in their relationships. Garland further mentioned that "Spiritual disciplines are the ways we intentionally and regularly open ourselves to God's working in and through us. They are ways we seek to move beyond living mindlessly on the surface of our routines. We use spiritual disciplines to open ourselves to experiencing and celebrating God in our round of daily activities. Just as consistent physical exercise results in a strengthened body, so spiritual discipline, over time, results in a strengthened faith".47

---

[47] Garland, *Family Ministry, A Comprehensive Guide* 235.

Conclusion

We embarked on a journey regarding the principles of a lifetime Christian marriage. The discussion has brought to the fore various Christian traditional theologians' definitions of marriage. They all seem to attest to the fact that, marriage is a covenantal bond between two opposite sex, man and woman, was established by God, and recognized by all human society as sacred for companionship, intimacy, procreation, and life long relationship. Critical reflections from the discussion point to the fact that the foundation or institution of marriage is from God, therefore, the necessary respect, and dignity should be rendered to him, and not to abuse the institution with human parochial interests and philosophies. Concerning the fundamental guiding principles in choosing a lifetime partner, we have come to understand that the choice of a partner should not be based on conditionality, and infatuation, but rather **true love** *(agape)*. The consideration of maturity readiness, the involvement of the vertical and horizontal resources – (God), and (family and church leadership) should be very paramount in terms of direction and divine blessings. The principles of the longevity of a Christian marriage such as oneness in holistic life of the couple's endeavors, the transparency that contributes to trust, adaptability because of one's diverse background, serving and forgiveness which should be the responsibilities for both couples, love and humility as the inevitable reciprocal mandate, social and economic welfare of their immediate families as a test of Christian faith, faithfulness/fidelity which embodies the very core of the marriage covenant relationship, communication as a unique tool to the sustainability of a lifetime relationship, and the couple's spirituality which seems to be the foundation upon which the marriage is built, serves as a pivot upon which marriage longevity stands. Moreover, we hope that this work would also serve as a tool to guide to-be-couples, married, and deficient married couples, and for vocational counselors for counseling purposes in the marriage life journey.

We shall conclude with the assertion of Jesus' words in the book of Matthew that, "Everyone then who hears these words of mine and does them will be like a wise man who built his house upon the rock; and the rain fell, and the floods came, and the winds blew and beat upon that house, but it did not fall, because it had been founded on the rock. And everyone who hears these words of mine and does not do them will be like a foolish man who built his house upon the sand, and the rain fell, and the floods came, and the winds blew and beat against that house, and it fell; and great was the fall of it (Matthew 7:24-27)". Jesus promised that if you build your marital life on the firm foundation of his words and counseling principles your life would stand even in a storm."[48]

---

[48] Peter Rhea Jones, Sr. "The Winds Will Blow: A Sermon on Matthew 7:24-27" *A Baptist Theological Journal Review & Expositor* 109 no 2 Spr. 2012, (Accessed on 1/9/20, at Amridge University Library), 287.

References

Adeyemo, Tokunboh. *Africa Bible Commentary, A One-Volume Commentary Written by 70 Africa Scholars.* Kenyan, Nairobi: Hippo Books, 2006.

Albert, Mohler R. God, Marriage, and the Family: Rebuilding the Biblical Foundation' Journal of the Evangelical Theological Society; Lynchburg Vol. 50, Iss. 1, (March 2007): 167-170. Accessed 1/13/20 at Amridge University library.

Barker, Kenneth L. *The Expositor's Bible Commentary,* Abridged Edition, New Testament. Grand Rapids, Michigan: Zondervan, 1994.

Cyril, Barber J. "Growth Counseling, Pt 1: Enriching Marriage and Family Life" *Journal of Psychology & Theology,* 2 no 4 Fall 1974, p 322-323. ATLA, Accessed 1/9/20), 322.

DeSilva, David A. *An Introduction to the New Testament, Context, Methods & Ministry Formation.* Downers Grove, Illinois: InterVarsity Press, 2004.

Don, Bissett. "A church-sponsored divorce recovery through a group experience." *Journal of Family Ministry* 4, no. 2 (1990). 45-53.

Douglas, J.D., and Tenney, Merrill C. *Zondervan Illustrated Bible Dictionary.* Grand Rapids, Michigan: Zondervan, 2011.

Garland, Diana R. *Family Ministry, A Comprehensive Guide.* Downers Grove, Illinois: InterVarsity Press, 2012.

Green, Joel B. *The Everyday Study Edition.* Dallas: Word Pub. 1996.

John, Patton. "Pastoral perspective on marriage and family counseling." *The Journal of Pastoral Care* 33, no. 1 (March 1979), 38-43.

Jones, Peter Rhea Sr. "The Winds Will Blow: A Sermon on Matthew 7:24-27" *A Baptist Theological Journal Review & Expositor* 109 no 2 Spr. 2012, (Accessed on 1/9/20, at Amridge University Library), 287.

Keener, Craig S. *The Gospel of Matthew: A Socio-Rhetorical Commentary*. Grand Rapids, Michigan: Wm. B. Eerdmans Publishing, 1999.

Longman, Tremper III. *The Baker Illustrated Bible Dictionary*. Grand Rapids, Michigan: Baker Publishing Group, 2013.

Marshall, Howard I. *New Testament Theology, Many Witnesses, One Gospel*. Downers Grove, Illinois: Intervarsity Press, 2004.

Seager, Colin Thane. "A Biblical Foundation Counseling Strategy to Direct Couples to Become One Flesh in Marriage," *Liberty University,* ProQuest Dissertations Publishing, 2014. 3644295. Accessed on 1/12/20 at Amridge University library.

Strauch, Alexander. *Biblical Eldership, An Urgent Call to Restore Biblical Church Leadership* (Littleton, CO: Lewis & Roth Publishers, 2016), 75.

Weise, Robert W. "Marriage the Divine and Blessed Walk of Life" *Concordia Journal,* 40 no 1Wint 2014, (Accessed on 1/9/2020 at Amridge University library), 46.

Williams, Joel S. "Ministry to Families and Individuals, lecture notes on Guilt and Forgiveness in Ministry and Pastoral Counseling." (Amridge University, 5/29/2020).

www.ingramcontent.com/pod-product-compliance
Lightning Source LLC
Chambersburg PA
CBHW030532080526
44586CB00011B/399